Words At Leisure

Bill Ridgway

Edward Arnold

Introduction

Although many people still work long hours in factories and offices, there is now much more of a chance to take part in leisure activities. These can be of many different kinds—a visit to the cinema, perhaps, or a football match, practising a sport, or having a hobby. Even attending an evening class. Different people have different ideas about what to do in their spare time. What might seem like work to some is a pleasure to others.

This book covers a wide range of leisure activities. Those who have read the other books in the English or the Maths series (*Read All About It*, *Words At Work*, *Maths About Town* etc.) will know how to tackle the exercises. All the chapters (except chapter 23) cover two pages, and they can be done in any order.

When you've finished you should know a bit more about leisure activities and the words used to describe them.

Acknowledgements

The publishers would like to thank the following for permission to include copyright material:

Bessacarr Prints (and Guidebooks); Derek lock Concert Promotions; Bord na Mona; Dinosaur Publications Limited; Martin Dockerty and Chris Randall for 'Concert for TV'; Evening Sentinel; The Lau School of Kung Fu; Leek College of Further Education; The Littlewoods Organisation plc; D B and H Murray; Pavilion Gardens; Razzamatazz at Jollees; The Reader's Digest Association Limited; Severn-on-Trent Water Authority; Smiths Happiway Spencers Ltd; Sportsmans Emporium; Stoke Original Theatre; Twinram Marine; Westminster Passenger Service Association and World International Publishing Limited.

© Bill Ridgway 1984

First published in Great Britain 1984 by
Edward Arnold (Publishers) Ltd,
41 Bedford Square, London WC1B 3DQ

British Cataloguing in Publication Data
Ridgway, Bill
    Words at leisure.
    1. Recreation—Great Britain
    I. Title
    306′.48′0941   GV75
    ISBN 0-7131-0861-4

Filmset in 11/13pt Compugraphic Century by CK Typesetters Ltd, Sutton, Surrey
Printed and bound by in Great Britain by Spottiswoode Ballantyne Ltd, Colchester and London

Contents

GROW YOUR OWN TOMATOES

Planting

Using SUREGROW bags tomatoes can be grown indoors in a greenhouse, conservatory or sun-lounge. They can also be grown outdoors on a balcony, patio or terrace preferably against a south or west facing wall or fence.

Indoors the SUREGROW bag will carry 3 plants to maturity. These should be planted 38 cm apart – one in the middle and one at each end.

INDOORS

OUTDOORS

They should not be stuck through the bottom of the bag. As commercial growers using these packs for early crops have achieved yields of up to 12 kilos per plant it is obvious that whatever means of support is used it must be strong enough to support a plant with a heavy weight of fruit.

Watering

For 2-3 weeks after planting very little water is required. Thereafter apply ¼ litre per plant daily increasing over 3-4 weeks to ½ litre per plant daily. As the plants mature and the fruit on the lower trusses swells the amount of water should be increased to 1 litre per plant daily. Regular and even watering is essential for success. Keep SUREGROW moist but never saturated.

Planting Time

The planting time will vary depending on whether the plants are being grown indoors or outdoors and, if indoors, on whether the area is heated or not. Some allowance must also be made for local climatic conditions e.g. in southern coastal areas planting could be done 2-3 weeks earlier than in cooler northerly inland areas. The following is a general guide.

Heated greenhouse/ conservatory etc.	– from Mid-March
Unheated greenhouse/ conservatory etc.	– from Mid-April
Outdoors	– late May

Support

As tomato plants develop they require support. This can be provided by training each plant up a string, mesh or cane. Tomato plants are not natural climbers so it is necessary to twist the string around the plants as they grow or tie them to the support at regular intervals. If canes are used they should be stuck in the ground beside the bag.

Feeding

Regular feeding is essential for a good crop. Any soluble or liquid proprietary tomato feed may be used. This should be applied in accordance with the manufacturer's instructions.

Commence feeding 2-3 weeks after planting indoors or 4 weeks after planting outdoors.

Fruit Setting

Fruit will develop only if the flowers are pollinated. This is normally done by insects (e.g. bees) which may not be sufficiently numerous or active with early indoor planting. Therefore to ensure pollination the trusses should be tapped daily as soon as the flowers have begun to open. A fairly moist atmosphere is necessary for successful pollination. In hot dry weather the plants should be sprayed with water to provide this. Alternatively indoors the floor or paths could be sprinkled with water. If this is not feasible large shallow dishes of water should be placed close to the plants.

In the Garden

People who like gardening might want to read the information given opposite. It tells you how to use soil-filled bags called 'Suregrow bags' to grow your own tomatoes.

Planting

A1 Copy and complete:
    a) Tomatoes can be grown in a _____, _____ or _____ _____.
    b) They can be grown outdoors on a _____, _____ or _____.
    c) It is best if a wall or a fence faces _____ or _____ if you want to grow outdoor tomatoes against it.

2 How many tomato plants can you put in a Suregrow bag if you are using it *indoors*? How far apart should they be planted?

Planting Time

3 Copy and complete:
    a) When you plant tomatoes will depend on whether you are growing them _____ or _____.
    b) When you plant tomatoes indoors will depend on whether the room is _____ or not.

4 Copy and match the words and phrases on the left with the meanings on the right:

some allowance must be made	land away from the sea
local climatic conditions	land near the sea
coastal areas	you must bear in mind
inland areas	the weather you get in a small area

5 Look at the general guide, then copy and complete the following:

Tomatoes can only be grown in mid-March if the greenhouse etc, is _____.

Support

6 What three things can you use to support a tomato plant?
7 Why must tomato plants be tied to the support?
8 Do you stick canes in the ground inside or outside the bag?
9 Why has a plant support got to be strong?
10 If you wish, draw the picture showing the bag, the plants, and some netting.

Watering and Feeding

11 How much water do tomatoes need
    a) 2–3 weeks after planting?
    b) after 4 weeks?
    c) when the fruit on the lower stems (trusses) swells?

12 Copy the words below and choose a meaning which fits from the three in brackets:
    Regular means (often/never/tomato).
    Essential means (forget/necessary/water).
    Soluble means (can be solved/powder/will dissolve).
    Proprietary means (named/pottery/proper).

Fruit Setting

13 What normally pollinates flowers?
14 There may not be many insects indoors. How should you pollinate the flowers then?

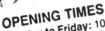
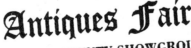
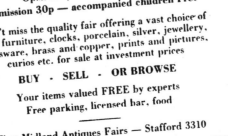
6

Out and About 1

The clips opposite were taken from a local paper. They show four places which you could visit in your spare time.

Roxy Roller Rink

A1 In which street would you find the Roxy Roller Rink?

2 In which town would you find the Roxy Roller Rink?

3 What are the opening times from Monday to Friday? Begin like this: 10 a.m.–11.45 a.m. etc.

4 Which sessions would the following people attend?
a) a woman who wants to lose weight
b) someone who wants to have a meal after skating

5 What are the Saturday and Sunday opening times? Begin like this: 9.45 a.m.–11.45 a.m. etc.

6 Look at Skate Shop. What is the least you would have to pay for Disco Roller Skates?

7 Name three Skate Accessories (things you could buy along with your skates).

The Trentham Classic

8 What game is being played?

9 Name the competitors.

10 What time does the bar open?

11 What word tells you there is food to be had?

12 How much is it to go in?

13 What number could you phone for more information?

Christmas at the Queens

14 Copy and complete using words from the list in brackets:
Live entertainment is (video and records/entertainment by performers).
Advance tickets are (tickets you buy before the night/expensive tickets).

15 On which days are the dances held? Between what times are the dances held?

16 Where are the dances held? What number would you phone to find out more?

17 On what November date do the dances start?

18 During what time of year will the dances take place?

Antiques Fair

Copy and complete this paragraph:
The Antiques Fair is held at the Stafford _____ Showground on _____ and Sunday, _____ 6th-7th. It is open daily from _____ a.m. to _____ p.m. and it costs _____ to go in. On sale will be fine _____, cl_____, si_____, je_____, glas_____, br_____, and pic_____. Items will be valued _____ by experts. For more information ring Stafford _____.

B1 Which of the four things opposite would you most like to visit or take part in? Say why.

2 Which of the four would you least like to visit or take part in? Say why.

8

Razzamatazz

'Razzamatazz' was the name given to a Stoke-on-Trent entertainments centre which was opened in 1982.

Look at the top section of the advertisement

A1 a) What are the hours of opening?
b) What does it cost to go in (admission)?
c) On what *three* days is it open for the 'Over Twenties'?

2 What two words tell you that the building was changed or altered when the new entertainments centre was built? (Clue letters: e_____ a_____)

3 Copy and complete this paragraph using the clue-letters given:
   Razzamatazz has these features: live e_____, sprung d_____ fl_____, _____ large bars, a superb b_____, a wine b_____ and a l_____ g_____ area.

4 Copy and match the words and meanings below:

bistro	comedians, singers etc.
live entertainment	floors which 'give' as you dance
sprung dance floors	a place to eat

5 If you were sixteen years of age, on which night would you go to Razzamatazz?

6 a) From what date is Razzamatazz open to teenagers?
b) At what time does the teenage session end?
c) How much would a teenager pay to go in?

Look at the top right section of the advertisement

7 What sort of clothing may be worn at Razzamatazz?
8 Write down the address and telephone number of the entertainments centre.

A Special Invitation for the Readers of the Evening Sentinel

9 Copy the following statements and write **true** or **false** at the end of each:
a) If you cut out the invitation you can go to Razzamatazz free on Thursday 4th and Friday 5th March.
b) If you cut out the invitation you can go to Razzamatazz free before 7.30 a.m. on Saturday 23rd April.
c) Everyone must wear a suit or a dance-dress.

B1 Copy and complete the paragraph below using words from the box:
   I have a great time at _____ on _____ night. It only costs _____ to go in, and I meet most of my friends there. There are so many things to do. I like _____ best, and when we have some money we go for something to _____ in the _____. My boyfriend likes dancing too, but he prefers to play _____ and video games.

> dancing, eat, pool, Wednesday, Razzamatazz, bistro, 50p

Electric guitars...

ARION GUITAR TUNER
E

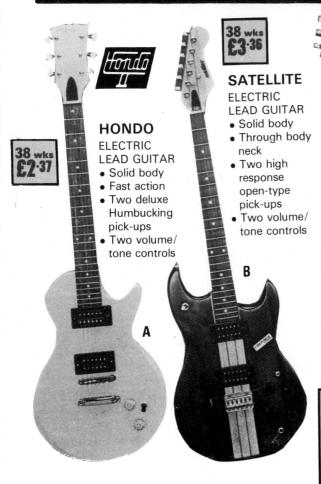

38 wks £3·36

SATELLITE
ELECTRIC LEAD GUITAR
- Solid body
- Through body neck
- Two high response open-type pick-ups
- Two volume/tone controls

B

38 wks £3·36

'KAY'
GUN-SHAPED ELECTRIC LEAD GUITAR
- Solid body
- Fast action
- Lightweight
- Through body neck
- Two super distortion pick-ups
- Three speed controls

HONDO
ELECTRIC LEAD GUITAR
- Solid body
- Fast action
- Two deluxe Humbucking pick-ups
- Two volume/tone controls

38 wks £2·37

A

38 wks £3·56
C

38 wks £2·64

'KAY'
ELECTRIC LEAD GUITAR
- Solid body
- Fast action
- Two pick-ups
- Four volume/tone controls

F

COLUMBUS AMPLIFIED MIXING HEADPHONES
D

A Single cutaway contoured mahogany body. 3-position selector switch. Adjustable bridge. Kit consists of bag, strap, plectrum and tutor book. Overall length 39 ins, width 9 ins, depth 1½ ins. **Screaming-yellow or racing-orange.** *Delivery normally within 28 days from receipt of order.*
PV 526 Guitar £89·99
    20 wks £4·50; 38 wks £2·37

B Rosewood-finished maple through neck of multiple laminated maple. Maple fingerboard. Selector switch. Integral bridge and tailpiece. Brass saddles. Supplied with cover, strap, tutor book and plectrum. Overall length 39 ins, width 10 ins, depth 1½ ins. *Delivery normally within 28 days from receipt of order.*
PV 506 Guitar £127·50
    20 wks £6·38; 38 wks £3·36

Not illustrated. Satellite electric bass guitar. All other details identical to item B except the overall length is 46 ins. *Delivery normally within 28 days from receipt of order.*
PV 509 Bass guitar £127·50
    20 wks £6·38; 38 wks £3·36

C Rosewood-coloured body. Brass top nut bridge and position markings on neck. Two selector switches. Complete with machine-gun style strap and padded carrying bag, tutor book and record. Jack plug socket. Overall length 34 ins, width 7 ins, depth 1½ ins. *Delivery normally within 28 days from receipt of order.*
PV 507 Guitar £135·00
    20 wks £6·75; 38 wks £3·56

D Columbus amplified mixing headphones. Built-in amplifier. Practice on any instrument requiring amplifier without disturbing others. Line input socket (complete with lead), separate volume, play with pre-recorded backing or accompaniment. Use as normal stereo headphones when guitar/line facility switched off. Takes one 9-volt battery. Black-orange.
PV 004 Guitar headphones £21·00
    20 wks £1·05

E Arion guitar tuner. High tuning accuracy. Built-in microphone and external input jack for meter tuning. Easy-to-read meter and indicator. Can be connected via amplifier for tuning by ear. Battery indicator. Operates from 9-volt battery. Height 2 ins, width 2½ ins, depth 4¾ ins.
PV 005 Guitar tuner £29·99 20 wks £1·50

F Black-coloured polyester-finished body, multiple bound white celluloid edges and head. Rhythm/treble selector switch. Fingerboard inlaid with celluloid position markers. Chromium-plated machine heads. Detachable neck with adjustable truss rod. Complete with neckcord, tutor book and record, plectrum and guitar bag. Overall length 40 ins, width 13 ins, depth 1½ ins. *Delivery normally within 28 days from receipt of order.*
PV 508 Guitar £99·99
    20 wks £5·00; 38 wks £2·64

This range has since been updated and prices are no longer current.

Buying a Guitar

The guitar has been a very popular instrument for more than thirty years. There are two main kinds—an electric guitar, which can have a solid body, and an acoustic guitar, which is hollow and gives a different sound. The page opposite shows only electric guitars.

Look at the illustrations

A1 Each guitar has a letter by it. What letter is:
   a) the Hondo guitar?
   b) the Satellite guitar?
   c) the Kay electric lead guitar?
 2 Write down the *letter* of the guitar these words apply to:
   a) three speed controls
   b) two de-luxe Humbucking pick-ups
   c) four volume/tone controls
 3 Write down the *name* of all the guitars these words apply to:
   a) solid body
   b) fast action
   c) two volume/tone controls
 4 Draw one of the guitars shown, and copy the specifications (information) given by the side of the guitar you have chosen.

Look at the information below the illustrations

5 **Guitar A**
   a) What wood is the body made from?
   b) What does the kit consist of?
   c) What are the guitar's measurements?
   d) What colours can you buy it in?
6 **Guitar B**
   Copy and complete using a word from the brackets:
   a) The guitar has a _____ wood (oak, maple, chestnut) fingerboard.

   b) The guitar has a _____ switch. (rejector, connector, selector)
   c) The guitar is sent with cover, _____, tutor book and plectrum. (strap, saddles, rosewood)
 7 **Guitar C**
   Copy and complete:
   a) The guitar has a r__sewoo__ coloured body.
   b) The position markings on the neck are in br__ss.
   c) The carrying bag is p__dded.
 8 **Guitar F**
   Copy and write **true** or **false** after each:
   a) The guitar has a red body.
   b) The guitar has a rhythm/treble selector switch.
   c) There are iron position markers.
   d) There is a neckcord.
 9 Two other items are advertised opposite, apart from guitars.
   a) What is item **D**?
   b) What is item **E**?

B1 Below are five statements. Write down the three which are said by someone who likes guitars.
   'If it wasn't for guitars pop music wouldn't be half as good.'
   'A guitar never sounds good unless it's part of a band.'
   'A guitar sounds good no matter what kind of music is being played.'
   'I hate rock and pop music and the instruments that make it.'
   'It costs a lot of money to buy a piano, but a second-hand guitar can give you good value for only a few pounds.'

LEISURE

Monday Leisure Pursuits

Class	Time	Tutor	Place
Woodwork	2.00-4.00	D. Smith	S. of A.
Amateur Photography (Adv.)	7.00-9.00	T. Silvester	L.C.F.E.
Beginners' Car Maint.	7.00-9.00	G. Minshall	L.C.F.E.
Beginners' Badminton	7.00-9.00	G. Foulkes	Mountside
Beginners' Guitar	7.00-9.00	C. Ellis	Russell Street
Dress	7.00-9.00	H. Birch	S. of A.
Embroidery	7.00-9.00	D. V. Barr	S. of A.
Hatha Yoga I	7.00-9.00	R. Barnacle	East Street
Hatha Yoga II	7.00-9.00	C. Lovatt	Milner Hall
Hostess Cookery I	7.00-9.00	J. Broome	L.C.F.E.
Men's Keep Fit I	8.00-9.30	C. Williamson	St. Edwards Hall
Painting	7.00-9.00	A. Rolph	S. of A.
Physically Handicapped Crafts	12.30-4.00	D. Owen	Red Cross
Pottery	7.00-9.00	S. R. Hansell	S. of A.
Women's Crafts	7.00-9.00	B. M. Hutchinson	S. of A.
Woodwork	7.00-9.00	D. Smith	S. of A.
Dressmaking	7.00-9.00	M. Salt	St. Edwards Cheddleton

1st Meeting Monday 14th September

PLEASURE

Tuesday Leisure Pursuits

Class	Time	Tutor	Place
Woodwork for Disabled	10.00-12.00	D. Smith	S. of A.
Physically Handicapped Crafts	10.30-3.00	D. Owen	Red Cross
Dress	1.00-3.00	H. Birch	S. of A.
Dress I	2.00-4.00	I. E. Sims	L.C.F.E.
Hatha Yoga III	1.45-3.15	C. Lovatt	L.C.F.E.
Woodwork	2.00-4.00	D. Smith	S. of A.
Painting	7.00-9.00	F. J. England	S. of A.
Photography	7.00-9.00	P. Rider	S. of A.
Beginners' Electronics	7.00-9.00	P. Smith	L.C.F.E.
Cordon Bleu Cookery	7.00-9.00	L. Savage	L.C.F.E.
Dress II	7.00-9.00	I. E. Sims	L.C.F.E.
Golf Coaching I★	6.30-7.30	P. Stubbs	L.C.F.E.
Golf Coaching II★	7.30-8.30	P. Stubbs	L.C.F.E.
Golf Coaching III★	8.30-9.30	P. Stubbs	L.C.F.E.
Guitar Intermediate	7.00-9.00	C. Ellis	L.C.F.E.
Modern Dance	7.30-9.00	S. Marsden	L.C.F.E.
Men's Keep Fit II	7.30-9.00	M. West	Milner Hall

1st Meeting Tuesday 15th September

★Golf commences

ENJOYMENT

ART & CRAFT – K. F. ALBROW

TIME

GOOD HEALTH

Wednesday Leisure Pursuits

Class	Time	Tutor	Place
Hostess Cookery II	1.00-3.30	J. Broome	L.C.F.E.
Tailoring	1.30-3.30	I. E. Sims	S. of A.
Woodwork	2.00-4.00	D. Smith	S. of A.
Beginners' Badminton II	7.00-9.00	V. Bailey	L.C.F.E.
Cake Icing and Sugar Craft★	7.00-9.00	H. Messham	St. Edwards Cheddleton
Freezer Cookery	7.00-9.00	L. Savage	Milner
Hatha Yoga IV	7.00-9.00	R. Barnacle	East Street
Hatha Yoga V	7.00-9.00	T. Massey	Milner
Painting	7.00-9.00	F. J. England	S. of A.
Photography	7.00-9.00	H. Prince	L.C.F.E.
Pottery	7.00-9.00	C. R. Adams	S. of A.
Seasonal Cookery★	7.00-9.00	J. Broome	L.C.F.E.
Woodwork	7.00-9.00	D. Smith	S. of A.

★Commences January 1982

1st Meeting Wednesday 16th September

GOOD FOOD

IMPORTANT
ENROLMENTS
NOW 2-8 p.m.
SEPTEMBER 7th, 8th & 9th

COMPANIONSHIP

FOREIGN LANGUAGES

1. Beginners' French	Tuesday 7.00-9.00	D. Briggs
2. Beginners' Continuation French	Tuesday 7.00-9.00	H. Frost
3. Intermediate French	Thursday 7.00-9.00	J. Thompson
4. Beginners' German	Wednesday 7.00-9.00	J. Thompson
5. Intermediate German	Monday 7.00-9.00	To be appointed
6. Spanish	Monday 7.00-9.00	E. Morris

ALL OTHER COURSES –

Learning and Leisure

Many people attend evening classes or courses in their spare time. The information opposite is from a leaflet called 'Living, Learning and Leisure' which shows the sort of subjects which could be studied at a College of Further Education.

Monday Leisure Pursuits

A1 Name the tutor (teacher) taking
a) woodwork
b) dressmaking
c) Hatha Yoga 1
d) beginners' car maintenance
e) embroidery
2 a) Write down *all* the classes which are held at the Leek College of Further Education (L.C.F.E.).
b) Write down *all* the classes which are taken at the School of Art (S. of A.).
3 Most classes are taught from 7.00 p.m. -9.00 p.m. (two hours).
a) Name the class which is taught for *less* than two hours.
b) Name the class which is taught for *more* than two hours.

Tuesday Leisure Pursuits

4 Write down the name of any tutor who is taking a class on Tuesday *and* on Monday, together with the subject he/she takes.
5 a) How many classes are held at he L.C.F.E. on Tuesday?
b) How many classes are held at the S. of A. on Tuesday?
6 Write down the classes which are held
a) from 7.00 p.m.-9.00 p.m.
b) from 10.00 a.m.-12 noon;
c) from 1.00 p.m.-3.00 p.m.

Wednesday Leisure Pursuits

7 What classes do the following tutors take:
a) V. Bailey   b) H. Prince
c) D. Smith   d) J. Broome
e) H. Messham?
8 a) Who takes a class which lasts for 2½ hours?
b) Who takes a class lasting for 2 hours, and ending at 3.30 p.m.?
9 Make a list of the classes held on Wednesday which were also held on Monday. Begin like this: Hostess Cookery. (Ignore I, II etc. after the name of the class.)

Foreign Languages

10 a) How many foreign languages can be taken?
b) How long does each foreign language class last?
11 Now find the word 'Enrolments' on the leaflet. (Enrolments means 'Signing on for a course and paying any necessary money.)
a) Between which hours can you enrol for a class?
b) On which dates can you enrol?

B   Copy the comments below and write after each one the name of the class the speaker might like to join.
'I like keeping fit.' (Bob)
'I like making clothes and sewing.' (Sandra)
'I like cooking.' (Sam)
'I like working with clay.' (Alice)
(Note: there can be more than one 'right' answer.)

KUNG FU

Swim for fitness

SWIMMING is the complete exercise. From birth to old age, it's about the best all-round exercise you can take. Water is the ingredient that makes swimming the closest thing to a perfect sport. Because your body is supported by water, your spine and joints can move more freely and it's a load off your back, hips, knees and feet, so it's ideal for older and disabled people as well as the young and active.

Swimming is also one of the only sports that tones every muscle in your body. If you swim regularly, your body stands a much better chance of keeping in shape.

If you're just an occasional swimmer, it's best to take things easy to start with. A length of the pool is further to swim than it looks, so work on widths. Swim with a smooth, easy relaxed stroke, take deep breaths in time with the action and don't swim so hard that you tire yourself.

Choose a swimsuit which has been specially designed for serious swimming—a leading company make a range which is excellent for comfort and a perfect fit. Try a variety of swimming styles—breast-stroke is good for hips and knees, back-stroke and crawl for shoulders and trunk.

But remember to get the most out of your swimming by avoiding a few common mistakes. Don't swim immediately after a heavy meal. Don't let yourself get too cold or you may get cramp, and don't swim where there are dangerous currents or tides.

And don't be put off if you can't swim. You can get lessons at your local pool, where there are probably classes for all ages and, if you prefer, private tuition can usually be arranged.

14

Keeping Fit

The two clips opposite are from a local paper. Each clip has information about a sport, and how this sport can help you to keep fit.

Kung Fu

A1 Kung Fu is a Chinese take-away/a Chinaman's name/a new kind of motor oil/a method of self defence. Which?

2 The advertisement lists some of the reasons why you might decide to go along to the gym to train. The first is 'tones up muscles'. What are the other three?

3 a) Tuition means teaching/learning/eating. Which?
 b) Martial Arts are art and craft/self defence/painting. Which?
 c) A system is a way or method/a tank in the attic/the opposite of a brother. Which?

4 Draw the figure. Write underneath your drawing the three branches of self-defence taught at the gym, beginning with Shoulin Kicking Techniques.

5 a) What do you think the letters B.K.F.C. stand for?
 b) What do you think M.A.C. stands for? ('Martial' is the first word.)

6 What other sort of training can be given?

7 What age group do the Self Defence and Keep Fit classes cater for?

8 On what day does training take place?

9 Write down the full name and address of the school of Kung Fu.

Swim for Fitness

10 Copy the writing below and use words from the first paragraph to complete it (clue-letters are given).
 Swimming is the best all-r_____ exercise you can take, because your b_____ is supported by w_____. Besides allowing your sp_____ and jo_____ to move freely, it can also take a load off your b_____ and f_____. Swimming is good for o_____ people and dis_____ people too.

11 Look at paragraph 2.
 a) Which parts of your body does swimming tone (improve)?
 b) How do you keep your body in shape?

12 Look at paragraph 3.
 a) What advice is the occasional swimmer given (the person who doesn't swim often)?
 b) What tip is given on breathing methods?

13 Look at the paragraph which begins 'Choose a swimsuit ... '
 a) What advice is given about choosing a swimsuit?
 b) What advice is given about swimming styles?

14 Look at the rest of the article. Then copy the following sentences down and write **true** or **false** after each:
 Always swim after a heavy meal.
 Always get yourself as cold as possible.
 Don't swim where there are dangerous currents or tides.
 You can't get lessons at your local pool.
 Private tuition can usually be arranged.

HEAVEN
VILLIERS STREET, LONDON WC2

HEY ELASTICA!

DANSE SOCIETY

MONDAY
15th NOVEMBER 9-30pm
All tickets £3.00

HAMMERSMITH ODEON

FASHION

KAJAGOOGOO

WEDNESDAY
10th NOVEMBER
7.30pm
TICKETS £3.75 £3.25

A CONCERT FOR TV

THURS. 11th NOV

ORANGE JUICE
+
ORCHESTRE JAZIRA

DOORS 8·00   ADMISSION £2·50   SHOW 8·45

AT THE **ACE** BRIXTON

(ON BRIXTON HILL, NEXT TO THE TOWN HALL)

TICKETS ON SALE AT:

L.T.B. SHAFTSBURY AVENUE
PREMIER BOX OFFICE
ROUGH TRADE RECORDS, KENSINGTON PARK ROAD W11
(off Portobello Road)

—OR ON THE DOOR ON THE NIGHT—

Pop Concerts

Going to a pop concert makes an enjoyable evening out and gives people a chance to see their favourite group in action. Opposite are three pop-concert posters for you to look at.

Look at 'Orange Juice'

A1 On which day will the concert be held?
 2 Who is performing with Orange Juice?
 3 What is the admission cost?
 4 What time do the doors open?
 5 What time does the performance begin?
 6 How long after the doors open does the performance begin?
 7 Where does the concert take place?
 8 What is the ACE, do you think?
 9 Where is the ACE?
 10 What building is next door to the ACE?
 11 Can tickets be bought at the door on the night?
 12 The address below shows where tickets are on sale. There are eight mistakes in the address. Copy it out properly:
    L.T.B. Shassbery Avenue
    Dreamers Box Ofice
    Ruff Trade Records
    Kennington Dark Road W12
    (off Belloporto Road)

Look at the other two posters

13 Name the two groups playing at the Hammersmith Odeon.
14 On what day are they playing?
15 On what date are they playing?
16 At what time are they playing?
17 What would two of the more expensive tickets cost?
18 What would two of the cheaper tickets cost?

19 Does the way Kajagoogoo is written make the music seem lively or dull? Why?
20 Write the address of Heaven, the other concert hall.
21 Name the two groups which are playing there.
22 At what time does the performance begin?
23 What would four tickets cost?
24 On which date are the groups playing?
25 Different styles of writing are used to attract your attention. Copy two words from the posters which show two different writing styles.

B1 Below are some comments about pop concerts. Copy each comment and write (for) or (against) at the end of each one.
a) People who go to pop concerts are only interested in trouble.
b) Pop concerts are too noisy.
c) Pop concerts help you keep up with what's happening in music today.
d) You meet friends at a pop concert who like the same music as you do.
e) Loud music can damage your ears, so I don't go.
f) Pop music is bad music.
g) You need a break sometimes, and a good concert provides it.
h) There's so much on tape nowadays, it's good to hear something live for a change.

FARAWAY FRIENDS

Lynn Merry is 15 years of age, and her hobbies are horse-riding, football, dancing and comics. Barry Manilow is her favourite singing star. Write to her at 7 Sticklepath Hill, Barnstaple, North Devon.

★

Betty Colley is 16. She likes The Nolans, and her favourite film-star is Roger Moore. She enjoys playing records and doing jig-saw puzzles. Betty would like a boy or girl penfriend aged about 15 or 16 from America. She lives at 'The Hollies', Cross Lane, Alsager, Cheshire.

★

Nancy Smith of 12 Kent Hill, Kingston 11, Jamaica, wishes to thank all those who replied to her pen-pal request. She says 'I was really surprised – there were so many.'

★

Anne Tomkinson would like a pen-pal from Norway. Anne is 14 years old, and her hobbies are scrabble, reading, playing the guitar and swimming. She likes Police and Status Quo. Write to her at 24 Brent's Close, Stone, Staffordshire.

★

Della Buxton, of 3 Mount Road, Blackley, Lancashire, has lost her pen-pal's address, but would like to hear from her. Mary Thompson of Newcastle, please get in touch!

ARE YOU THERE?

I am trying to get in touch with a girl who used to live near me. Her name is Josephine Hodgkiss, and she went to Beech Comprehensive School. She moved in July. She had a brother named John and a sister named Jenny. Please write, Josephine.

Deborah Kelly, 25 Park View, Northwich, Cheshire.

◆◆◆◆

The Sleeping Deer

In the shadows of the night,
Lies a little fallow deer,
And his home is out of sight,
Hidden in the forest near.

In the dark he has no fear,
Dogs and men are far away,
But when morning's light is near,
The huntsman's horn will greet
   the day.

Through the trees the moon peeps
   down,
Branches rustle in the breeze,
And though the night is full of
   sounds
He sleeps and dreams beneath the
   trees.

He dreams in shadows of the
   night,
Where the little fallow deer
Has his home – it's out of sight
Hidden in the forest near.

Alice Jill Wilson,

Newcastle-on-Tyne.

ONLY DREAMING

I am always day-dreaming. It gets me into a lot of trouble at home and at school. Only the other day my teacher asked me to take some notes about Mary, Queen of Scots, and I wrote 'Mary, Queen of Spots' because I was thinking of a big pimple I had on my chin at the time.

Do any other readers live in a day-dream world like me, I wonder? I hope I'm not the only one.
          Leslie Birks,
          Weymouth, Dorset.

Hunting The Whale

I want to bring the readers' attention to the continuing practice of whale-hunting.

Although many countries no longer hunt this magnificent creature, and others take only a small number each year, in Japan and Russia whaling is still big business. Whale meat can be bought in the shops and blubber is sold for cosmetics – especially lipstick.

Whales are intelligent animals. They are the largest creatures that have ever lived, and they are in danger of being wiped out altogether. Certain kinds of whale – like the Blue Whale, for example – are now so few in number that there are hardly enough left to breed.

There is no reason to kill whales now. Other products can be used instead of whale blubber and whale oil.

Anyone who feels, as I do, that the whale should be allowed to live in peace can obtain more information from the address below.
    Please help.
      Time is running out.
      Save The Whale

Pamela Lissack, Grantham.

Reading a Comic Postbag

There are many different comics for sale covering a wide range of ages and tastes. Opposite is a typical page of readers' letters from a comic.

Faraway Friends

A1 Write down Lynn Merry's address.
  2 Does Lynn Merry have a favourite singing star?
  3 Who lives at 24 Brent's Close, Stone, Staffordshire?
  4 Who lives at 'The Hollies', Cross Lane, Alsager, Cheshire?
  5 How old is Anne Tomkinson?
  6 List Betty Colley's hobbies.
  7 Which group does Betty like?
  8 What would Anne Tomkinson like?
  9 Which pop-groups does Anne Tomkinson like?
10 Who was 'really surprised'?
11 List Anne Tomkinson's hobbies.
12 Who is 16 years of age?
13 List Lynn Merry's hobbies.

Keep us Posted

14 What does Deborah Kelly (Are You There?) want Josephine Hodgkiss to do?
15 Read the poem 'The Sleeping Deer'.
  a) What kind of deer is it? (verse 1)
  b) Why is the deer's home out of sight? (verse 1)
  c) Why isn't the deer frightened at night? (verse 2)
  d) What sort of dogs are they in verse 2 do you think?
  e) When will the huntsman sound his horn? (verse 2)
  f) What makes the branches rustle? (verse 3)

16 Read the letter 'Hunting the Whale'. Copy and complete, using words from the box below:

Most countries no longer hunt the _____, but in Japan and _____ whale-hunting is still big _____. These animals are _____ and should not be killed. Other products can be used instead of whale _____ and whale oil.

> intelligent, blubber, Russia, whale, business

B1 Below are nine statements. Five agree with killing animals for sport, or for making cosmetics and four do not. Copy each statement and write (agree) or (do not agree) at the end of each.
  a) Animals have no other purpose than to serve man.
  b) If animals were not killed for cosmetics, cosmetics firms would have to close and people would be put out of work.
  c) Scent made from animals is cheaper and better.
  d) Killing animals for cosmetics is not necessary, when other things can be used.
  e) If an animal has to be killed to make cosmetics, they should stop making cosmetics.
  f) Animals which are put to death die without pain.
  g) No one knows the harm killing wild animals will do to nature.
  h) Animals are only killed to make money for somebody.
  i) All men need sport, and hunting is only sport.

COMMON VARIETIES OF TROPICAL FISH

NAME	NATIVE LAND	LENGTH in cm	TEMPERATURE in degrees Centigrade	COLOURING	REMARKS
Angel Fish	Brazil	15	21–29	Brightly-coloured with vivid orange eyes.	Kite-shaped; do best in acid water.
Beacon Fish or Head-and-Tailight Fish	Northern South America	4.5	21–29	Silver yellow with shiny red over eyes and tail.	Breed well; need extra live food.
Blood Fin or Red-Tail	Argentina	4.5	15–27	Silver with red on fins.	Hardy; have been bred.
Buchanan's Dwarf Perch Fish	India and Burma	Varies	24–29	Varies.	Feed them live food only.
Coat of Mail Catfish	Argentina and Brazil	7	15–21	Yellow with a few green scales and golden eyes.	Whiskered, like all catfish.
Dwarf Gourami or Dwarf Rainbow Fish	Northern India	5	21–29	Blue with red stripes.	Beautiful; easy to keep; nest builders.
Guppy, Rainbow, or Millions Fish	Trinidad, Guiana, and Venezuela	3 (Male) 6 (Female)	18–37	Every colour of the rainbow	Most popular and hardy of tropicals.
Leopard Corydoras or Leopard Catfish	Brazil	6.5	15–27	Spotted leopard-like markings.	Hardy.
Molly or Sail-Fin	Gulf of Mexico	5–7.5	24–27	Varies greatly.	Do best in alkaline water.
Moonfish or Blotched Cyprinodont	Mexico	3.5 (Male) 5 (Female)	18–32	Blue, black, and gold varieties.	Good mixers; like green water; breed with other varieties.

Keeping Fish

Many people take an interest in tropical fish and spend quite a lot of their free time and their money looking after them. The table opposite gives the names of a number of these fish, together with the name of the area from which they come, their length and colouring. The water temperature each fish prefers is also important and this information is given in column four.

Look under NAME and NATIVE LAND

A1 Give the native land for each of the following:
   a) Coat of Mail Catfish
   b) Moonfish
   c) Angel Fish
   d) Leopard Catfish

2 a) Name the fish which come from the waters of Brazil.
  b) Name the fish which come from the waters of Argentina.
  c) Name the fish which come from India.

3 Give another name for:
   a) Beacon Fish
   b) Blood Fin
   c) Dwarf Gourami
   d) Guppy (two other names)
   e) Molly

Look under NAME, NATIVE LAND and LENGTH

4 How long can the following fish be?
   a) Angel Fish
   b) Coat of Mail Catfish
   c) Molly
   d) Guppy (male)
   e) Blood Fin

5 a) How long is the fish from the Gulf of Mexico?
  b) How long is the fish from Northern India?

Look at NAME and TEMPERATURE

6 Name the fish that prefer the following temperatures:
   a) 21°C-29°C
   b) 18°C-32°C
   c) 24°C-29°C
   d) 18°C-37°C

7 What water temperatures do the following fish prefer?
   a) Leopard
   b) Coat of Mail Catfish?

Look at NAME, COLOURING and REMARKS

8 What colour are the following fish?
   a) Beacon Fish
   b) Dwarf Gourami
   c) Blood Fin
   d) Moonfish
   e) Coat of Mail Catfish

9 Name the fish that:
   a) are good mixers
   b) are kite-shaped
   c) are easy to keep
   d) are whiskered
   e) do best in acid water
   f) do best in alkaline water

10 What *remarks* are made about?
   a) Leopard Catfish
   b) Blood Fin or Red-Tail

B1 Make a list of the things you would need to buy (apart from fish) if you were thinking of keeping fish as a hobby.

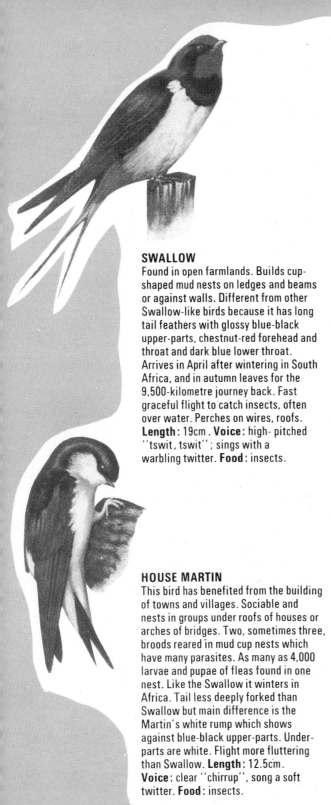

SWALLOW

Found in open farmlands. Builds cup-shaped mud nests on ledges and beams or against walls. Different from other Swallow-like birds because it has long tail feathers with glossy blue-black upper-parts, chestnut-red forehead and throat and dark blue lower throat. Arrives in April after wintering in South Africa, and in autumn leaves for the 9,500-kilometre journey back. Fast graceful flight to catch insects, often over water. Perches on wires, roofs. **Length:** 19cm. **Voice:** high-pitched ''tswit, tswit''; sings with a warbling twitter. **Food:** insects.

HOUSE MARTIN

This bird has benefited from the building of towns and villages. Sociable and nests in groups under roofs of houses or arches of bridges. Two, sometimes three, broods reared in mud cup nests which have many parasites. As many as 4,000 larvae and pupae of fleas found in one nest. Like the Swallow it winters in Africa. Tail less deeply forked than Swallow but main difference is the Martin's white rump which shows against blue-black upper-parts. Under-parts are white. Flight more fluttering than Swallow. **Length:** 12.5cm. **Voice:** clear ''chirrup'', song a soft twitter. **Food:** insects.

SWALLOW

DATE 8th April

TIME 10.30 a.m.

PLACE South Stack

WEATHER Fine, sunny, but cold N. Wind

NOTES Birds numbering 20+ were seen flying along rocky coast-line heading north. Are without doubt on migration from the south.

HOUSE MARTIN

DATE 21st April

TIME 2.00 p.m.

PLACE Llyn Llanwnan, Wales

WEATHER Cold n. wind. Clear & sunny

NOTES 25 or so birds seen over lake, hawking for insects. Recently arrived from their winter home in Africa.

Bird Watching

Bird-Watching is an interesting hobby, and many people take holidays in areas where may different kinds are to be found in the hope they can spot a bird they have never seen before.

Look at the Swallow

A1 Copy the picture of the swallow.
 2 a) Where is the swallow found?
   b) What are its nests made of?
   c) Where does it build them?
   d) What colour are its upper-parts?
   e) What colour is its forehead?
 3 Copy and complete:
   a) The swallow arrives from S__ __th
   Afr__ __a in Ap__ __ __.
   b) It goes back to Africa in the
   aut__ __n.
   c) The journey is 9,5__ __
   kil__m__tr__ __, and it catches
   in__ __ __ts on the way back.
   d) It is __ __ cm. long and makes the
   sound t__w__t, t__w__t.

Look at the House Martin

 4 Copy the picture of the house martin.
   Copy and match the words on the left
   with the meanings on the right.

benefited	insects or animals which live on another bird or animal
sociable	cases around maggots before they change to fleas
parasites	done well out of
pupae	likes to be with others

 5 Copy out the sentences below and
   write **true** or **false** after each one:
   a) The house martin nests under house
   roofs or arches.
   b) Twelve broods of young are reared in nests made of twigs.
   c) It winters in Alaska.
   d) The house martin has a white rump.
   e) Underparts are white.
 6 How long is the house martin?

Look at the written information

 7 On what date did the bird-watcher
   a) see the swallow?
   b) see the house martin?
 8 At what time did the bird-watcher
   a) see the swallow?
   b) see the house martin?
 9 At what place did the bird-watcher
   a) see the swallow?
   b) see the house martin?
10 Which bird
   a) was seen flying along a rocky coast-line?
   b) was seen over a lake?
11 Which bird
   a) arrived from its home in Africa?
   b) is on migration from the south?

B1 Below are ten words or phrases. Write
   down the ones which apply to bird-watching.
   a) open-air
   b) taking photographs
   c) watching television
   d) out-door
   e) doing a crossword puzzle
   f) wearing warm clothing
   g) taking notes
   h) binoculars
   i) no interest in nature
   j) indoors

GANDEY'S CIRCUS

Northern England's Greatest

BIDDULPH
MILL HAYES SPORTS GROUND
TUES MARCH 16th-SUN 21st

WEEKDAYS 4.45 & 7.45
SAT 2.00 & 4.45 SUN 3.00 ONLY
ADVANCE BOOKINGS
BIDDULPH TRAVEL CENTRE,
56 HIGH ST, BIDDULPH.
TEL S.O.T. 513311
OR ON CIRCUS SITE FROM
10.00 am – 3.00 pm FROM FIRST DAY OF VISIT

featuring MARY
CHIPPERFIELDS
EXOTIC ANIMALS

CAMELS * ZEBROID *
BLACK BEARS *
INDIAN ELEPHANT *
SHIRE HORSE *PYTHONS *
SHETLAND PONIES *
LLAMAS *

	SIDE TIER	FRONT	CHAIRS	RING SIDE
ADULT	£1.50	£2.00	£2.50	£3.50
CHILD/OAPS	£1.00	£1.50	£2.00	£2.50

PLUS ★

ALL STAR CIRCUS SUPERSHOW

D.Simpson '80

Come to the Circus!

Some circuses have had to close, but a number still tour Britain and Europe and it is not unusual even in these days of television to find the Big Top full. The poster opposite is for Gandey's Circus, one of the oldest in the British Isles.

A1 a) In which town was the circus held? (Bid__ __ __ __ __)
   b) At which ground was it held?
   c) Between which dates was it held?

 2 a) At what two times are the weekday performances?
   b) If the performances last for two hours, when does each performance finish?

 3 a) What are the Saturday performance times?
   b) What time is the Sunday performance?
   c) At what times will Saturday's performances finish?

 4 a) Where can you book beforehand (advanced bookings) to go to the circus?
   b) What is the telephone number of the Biddulph Travel Centre (S.O.T. means Stoke-on-Trent.)
   c) Where else can I book tickets for the circus? Between what times?

 5 Name the person who is in charge of the animals.

 6 Exotic means from other countries/ nervous/lions. Which?

 7 List some of the animals to be seen in the circus. Put them down in alphabetical order. Begin with 'black bears'.

Look at the prices chart at the bottom of the poster

 8 a) Which seats are the most expensive (Side Tier, Front etc.)
   b) Which seats are the cheapest?

 9 a) What would an adult pay for a *front* seat?
   b) What would a child pay for a *ring side* seat?
   c) What would an OAP (Old Age Pensioner) pay for a *chair*?

B1 Give the total cost of
   a) 3 adult's *ring side* seats
   b) 4 OAP's *side tier* seats
   c) 6 *front* seats for children
   d) 12 *chairs* for children and OAPs

 2 Copy and complete the paragraph below:

   We decided we would go to the 3.00 p.m. performance on _____ day. We booked in advance through the Biddulph _____ Centre. There were five of us going altogether: Mum, dad, grandma and my brother and I. (He is 9, and I'm 15.) We sat in *front* seats, and paid _____ altogether.

 3 Copy and complete the paragraph below (using words from the box).

   We enjoyed the _____ games and everyone thought they were very funny. The best performance was on the _____ _____ but the animals did very well too. Especially the _____. It's surprising what tricks such huge beasts can perform. We'll go again next _____.

year, high-wire, elephants, clown's

Stoke Original Theatre presents

TITANIC

by

RICHARD HOWELLS

Produced & Directed by

RAY JOHNSON

A dramatised documentary presented
on the <u>70th Anniversary</u> of the
greatest disaster in maritime history
(April 14th, 1912), and of its gallant
captain, Edward Smith (of Hanley).

Presented at

THE FORUM THEATRE

(CITY MUSEUM AND ART GALLERY)

Bethesda Street, Hanley.

on

WED, APRIL 14th, 1982 AT 7.30pm.
TICKETS: £1.50 (Children, O.A.Ps, Students 90p)
AVAILABLE
FROM THE MUSEUM OR PHONE 658976

Going to the Theatre

At one time theatres were packed almost every night of the week, but as other kinds of entertainment became important (such as TV, cinema etc.) many people began to lose interest in them. However, a number of theatres have made a comeback in recent years, and people who would once have stayed at home can sometimes be seen in the 'front row'.

A1 What is the name of the theatre where the play is being performed? (Look towards the bottom of the page.)

2 What is the name of the play?

3 What is the name of the playwright (the person who wrote the play)?

4 Copy and complete using words from the play-sheet:
   'Prod__c__d by' means got everything to do with the play together (scenes, script, props etc.).
   'Direc__ __d' by means showed the actors what to do.

5 Who produced and directed the play?

6 Copy and match:

a dramatised documentary is	the return of a certain date each year
an anniversary is	brave
maritime means	a play about a real event
gallant means	to do with the sea

7 On which date did the Titanic disaster happen?

8 Name the captain of the Titanic, and the town from which he came.

9 Where would you find the Forum Theatre?

10 a) On which date is the play being presented?
   b) At which time does the play begin?

11 What is the cost of
   a) an adult's ticket?
   b) a child's ticket?

12 a) Where can tickets be bought?
   b) Which number can you phone for tickets?

B1 Copy and complete using words from the opposite page:
   Mr. and Mrs. Jones took their two ch_____, George and Alice, to the th_____ to see the T_____. It cost them £_____ each for two adults and _____p each for the children, which was £_____ altogether.

2 Make out a play-bill like the one opposite using this information:
   House of Terror
   by Jacky Matthews
   Produced and Directed by Alan Gosforth
   Presented at The New Player's Theatre, Bryan Street, Shelford
   on Wed May 12th 1982 at 7.45 p.m.
   Tickets £1.25 (Children, O.A.P.s, Students 75p)
   Available from Theatre ticket office or phone 62628

3 Draw a small picture of the house of terror to fit the information (like the life-belts in the play-sheet opposite).

50 years a canoeist

DONALD BEAN, still paddling his own canoe after 50 years in the sport, races towards the finish during the Stafford and Stone Club's recent speed race.

Mr. Bean, who admits to being "turned 60," took up the sport during 1932 and this year celebrates his own golden jubilee by continuing to compete regularly.

The two and a half miles sprint from Darlaston Inn to Westbridge Park was not the kind of event in which Mr. Bean expects to excel and he was further handicapped by the use of an ultra-modern lightweight canoe.

"It is a very strenuous event and the canoe, while being excellent in a straight line, does not go round corners easily," he says. "I had no practice and must have finished somewhere near the last.

"Although I do not do well in this kind of event, I enjoy it and must be one of the oldest active paddlers in the Midlands."

Bargain

Mr. Bean's introduction to the sport was the result of a "bargain buy."

When the Stafford boat house was moved to near the Doxey-road bridge because the river was too shallow, Mr. Bean was on hand to purchase one of the old canoes.

"They were the old, heavy, open boats, but I used to spend most weekends and many holidays on the water, developing my interest by touring rivers and canals," he says.

His sport was interrupted by six years service in the British Army during the war, but Mr. Bean, who lives in Corporation-street, Stafford, was soon back on the water once he returned to civvie street.

When Stafford and Stone Canoe Club was formed by national coach Ken Langford in March, 1973, he was one of the early members.

"I am not interested in competitive sport, which is mainly for the youngsters, but I still enjoy the touring side," he says. "In January I led a tour of the River Churnet and while the snow was melting we all had a swim. It is also traditional to finish up in the river on New Year's Day and I rolled twice then.

"I am certain I am the oldest white water canoeist in the Midlands competing today, but I do it because I enjoy the sport. There is a danger element and 12 months ago I was at Llangollen when a club member was drowned on the swollen River Dee."

On the Water

The two clips opposite are from a local paper. They show two of the many ways in which people can enjoy their spare time 'on the water'.

Tittesworth Trout Fishing

A1 When does the season start?

2 How much is a permit (or licence) to fish?

3 a) Where can you write or call for further information (two places)?
b) Where can you phone for further information (two places)?

4 Who do you make postal orders or cheques payable to?

5 S.A.E. stands for Send Another Envelope/Stamped Addressed Envelope. Which?

6 What do all permit holders require?

50 years a canoeist

7 Copy and complete using a word or words from the list in brackets:
a) Donald Bean has been canoeing for _____ years. (50/20/10)
b) The speed race was held by the _____. (London Club/Stafford Club/Stafford and Stone Club)
c) Mr. Bean took up the sport in _____. (1923/1932/1392)
d) 'Celebrates his golden jubilee' means _____. (he celebrates 50 years as a canoeist/he celebrates at the Golden Jubilee pub/he wins some gold)

8 How far is it from Darlaston Inn to Westbridge Park?

9 What kind of canoe was Mr. Bean paddling?

10 What is it that the canoe *does not do* easily?

11 Where did Donald Bean come in the race?

Look under 'Bargain'

12 Copy and complete:
Mr. Be__n was on hand to
p__ __chase one of the old can__ __s.
They were old, h__ __vy, open boats.
He used to spend week__ __ds and
hol__d__ys on the water, touring
riv__ __ __ and can__ls.

13 Was Mr. Bean in the RAF, the navy or the army?

14 What is his address?

15 Civvie Street means being in the army/being out of the army. Which?

16 a) Who formed Stafford and Stone Canoe Club?
b) When was it formed?

17 a) What happened in January?
b) What happened on New Year's Day?
c) What happened on the River Dee?

B1 Make a list of all the sports and pastimes you can think of which make use of water.

Vale player has mumps

PORT VALE have been robbed of the services of key midfield player Geoff Hunter at the time when they are attempting to revive their promotion prospects.

Hunter, an ever-present in the league team this season, has contracted mumps and is likely to miss the remainder of Vale's crucial games this month.

"The jinx is still with us," exclaimed manager John McGrath preparing for tonight's visit to fifth-placed Peterborough.

"Just as we get one player back after three weeks in Terry Armstrong we lose another in Hunter and these are the types of players we need. It could hardly happen at a worse time considering the games we have to play."

Vale also have doubts about Jimmy Greenhoff at Peterborough and took a squad of 14 players to the London Road ground.

Gerry Keenan, who was left out in last Saturday's goalless home draw against Bury, is certain to return and there is a chance, too, that Peter Farrell will play.

Farrell has just completed a fortnight's suspension for allegedly showing a lack of effort in a reserve game

Also included is Trevor Brissett and Andy Shankland, who was withdrawn from the England Youth training squad at Lilleshall this week.

Stiff test

Vale badly need to string together some good results but in Peterborough they again face strong opposition.

Peterborough were the last team to win at Vale Park last October and they will be determined to complete the double as victory could take them into second spot.

Ace striker Robbie Cooke, with 24 goals this term, has scored eight times in his last five outings as Peterborough have put together a run of 10 games without defeat.

Vale have a reasonable record at Peterborough. They have lost on only one of their last nine visits but illness and injury clearly make the task of keeping it going even harder in a match they really need to win.

At the Match

Football is the most popular game ever in terms of the numbers of people who either go to a match each week or watch from their armchairs. The clip opposite is about Port Vale, a small Midlands football club.

Look at the first part of the article down to the heading 'Stiff test'

A1 Copy and complete using one of the meanings in brackets:
a) A key player is (a player with a key/an important member of the team).
b) To revive their promotion prospects means (to play well/to think again about the chances of going higher).
c) Contracted mumps means (has a licence/has caught mumps).
d) A jinx is (good luck/another word for 'drinks'/bad luck).

2 Copy and complete using *one* of the groups of words in brackets:
a) Geoff Hunter } is a key midfield
   John McGrath } player.
b) Geoff Hunter } has mumps.
   John McGrath }
c) Geoff Hunter } is the manager.
   John McGrath }
d) Port Vale } is in fifth place.
   Peterborough }

3 Name the player Port Vale got back after three weeks.
4 How many players did Vale take to the London Road ground, Peterborough?
5 What was the result of last Saturday's game against Bury?
6 Why was Farrell suspended for a fortnight?

Look at the second part of the article after the heading 'Stiff test'

7 a) What was the last team to win at Vale Park?
b) In which month did they win?
8 a) How many goals has Robbie Cooke scored this term?
b) How many games have Peterborough played without defeat?
9 Copy the sentences below, and write **true** or **false** at the end of each one:
a) Vale have had a very poor record at Peterborough.
b) They have lost on three of their last eight visits.
c) Illness and injury make the task of keeping the record going even easier.
d) They really need to win the match.

B1 Write a paragraph about your favourite outdoor sport. It need not be about football. Say why you like this sport more than any other.

Out and About 2

The clips opposite are from a newspaper. They give information about local events.

Yesteryear Rally

A1 Which association is putting on the event (see top of clip)?

2 In which park is the event being held?

3 During which two dates is the event being held?

4 Copy and complete using *one* of the words in brackets:

The gates open at _____ a.m. (9/10/11) on Saturday and at _____ a.m. (9/10/11) on Sunday. It costs _____ (£1/£2/£1.50) for adults and _____ (£5/50p/5p) for children.

5 Below are a list of ten attractions. Copy them down, then underline the ones shown in the clip.

shire horses, railway, military vehicles, balloons, fairground organs and rides, steam engines, model cars, airplanes, vintage cars and motor-cycles, fishing

Scramble

6 Which club is organizing the event?

7 Copy the writing below, but correct the underlined mistakes:

The scramble takes place on <u>Friday</u>, September <u>14</u>th at Cotton, near Alton House. Racing <u>ends</u> at 12 noon. There are refreshments, <u>paid</u> car-parking and toilets. The event is backed or sponsored by D.K.<u>M</u>. Motorcycles, <u>Manchester</u>.

Bavarian Gala Night

8 On what day is the Bavarian Gala night?

9 Where does the gala night take place?

10 How much are the tickets?

11 Name one of the guest artists from Granada TV's The Comedians.

12 a) Give the date of the Bavarian Gala Night.
b) Give the time you should arrive (reception).
c) Give the time the performance begins.
d) Give the telephone number you ring to book.

13 a) Write the address of the Clayton Lodge Hotel.
b) Look closely at the clip and say what will be provided.

14 Match the words on the left with their meanings on the right:

a gala is	will be remembered
Bavaria is	that the audience will take part
memorable means	part of Germany
audience partici-pation means	a show or festival

B1 Write a paragraph saying which of the events opposite you would most like to attend. Say why.

Boys with big aim

SCHOOLBOYS Ronan Shaw and Richard Bailey hope to beat the current depression by hitting the bullseye with a £5,000 competition between the world's top three darts stars.

The 16-year-old Endon High School pupils have no intention of job hunting when they leave school this summer.

Instead they aim to launch a new company on the financial success of their first plunge into business, a supreme darts challenge featuring world champion Jocky Wilson and former title-holders Eric Bristow and John Lowe.

A spokesman for Wilson and Bristow said that while they were interested in any competition featuring a £5,000 top prize, they would want "a cast iron guarantee" that the money would be available.

Bristow's agent said he had received a "tentative inquiry" and described such a tournament as "an interesting proposition."

The agent said he has already expressed doubt about the stars playing on a winner-take-all basis and added that it would be awkward to get the world's three best players in the same place on the same date.

Mr. Ron Glover, who manages the world champion, said he had been approached by a new company and did not realise the organisers were schoolboys.

"The maximum we have had in such challenges is £2,000 and I doubt whether they could find £5,000," he said. "I would want cast iron guarantees and will treat this very carefully."

The potential whiz kids have booked The Mayfair in Burslem for the tournament in the second week in July.

Spokesman for the pair, Ronan, of 101, Leek-road, Stockton Brook, is a prefect at Endon High School, where his co-partner, Richard, of Blue Bricks, Station-road, Endon, is head boy.

Ronan says: "I leave school in May and take my "O" levels in June, so they will obviously suffer while I am organising the tournament, but I aim to be self-sufficient when I leave school and to work for myself. We have both discussed it with our parents.

who are supporting us in this venture.

"We have put up £500 each and are sending out letters to nine top companies in the area seeking support with sponsorship. The whole thing has been costed out and we reckon it will cost up to £11,000. The sale of the tickets and television coverage should produce a profit.

"We are planning a two-day event, with all three players meeting each other on the Friday, then the top points scorers challenging for the £5,000 on Saturday night."

Mayfair acting general manager Mr. Chris Burns said the boys' efforts were genuine and The Mayfair were doing everything to assist, including reducing the hire charge.

Darts

Darts used to be a game played in a small room at the back of a pub. Nowadays the stakes are much higher, and international darts competitions attract large crowds—as well as television cameras.

A1 a) Who are the two schoolboys?
b) How much would the competition be worth?
c) What game will they be playing?
d) Which school are the boys from?
2 Name a) the world champion darts player, and b) the former title-holders.
3 What guarantee do Wilson and Bristow want?
4 'Tentative' means not fully worked out yet/like an octopus. Which?
5 What would be awkward?
6 a) Who manages the world champion?
b) What did Mr. Ron Glover *not* realise?
7 Copy and complete using words from the box below:
    The two whiz kids have booked _____ _____ in _____ for the _____ in the _____ week in _____.

> July, The Mayfair, Burslem, second, tournament

8 a) Who is the spokesman for the pair?
b) Where does he live?
c) What position does he hold at school?
d) What is the head boy's *surname*?
9 a) What examinations will Ronan be taking in June?
b) Copy the words from the article which mean that the boys' parents agree with their plans.
10 a) How does £500 come into the article?
b) How does £11 000 come into the article?
c) How does 'profit' come into the article?
11 Copy and complete using *one* of the words in brackets:
    They are planning a (one/two/three) day event, with all (one/two/three) players meeting each other on the (Monday/Friday/Wednesday), then the (top/bottom/middle) scorers challenging for the (£50/£500/£5000) on (Sunday/Saturday/Monday) (evening/night/morning).
12 Name one of the things The Mayfair was doing to help the boys.

B1 Write a paragraph about your favourite indoor sport, or a game you can play at home. It need not be about darts. Say why you like this sport more than any other.

A Home Cycle Exerciser. One for the whole family. Compete with speedometer/distance recorder and timer with alarm ————— ONLY **£109.95** (plus £5 carriage).

B Home Rower. Designed and developed for many years of continual use in the home. Variable resistance for fitness training. Stores in a vertical position ——————— ONLY **£99.95** (plus £5 carriage).

E Executive-Ergometer Cycle. Specially developed in co-operation with Finnish medical science experts. 1-60 min timer with alarm, rev counter, speedometer and variable pedal resistance for fitness training. Folds away for easy storage ——— ONLY **£159.95** (plus £5 carriage).

G Chromium Plated Dumbells. Improve fitness and muscle strength. Top quality dumbells from one of Europe's leading manufacturers. Buy any four pairs and receive a wooden stand FREE.

Weight	Price	Carr.
1 kgs pair	**£14.75**	(£1.00)
2 kgs pair	**£17.20**	(£1.00)
3 kgs pair	**£18.90**	(£1.50)
4 kgs pair	**£21.55**	(£2.00)
6 kgs pair	**£37.10**	(£2.50)
8 kgs pair	**£39.25**	(£3.00)
9 kgs pair	**£45.25**	(£3.50)
10 kgs pair	**£52.20**	(£4.00)

C Executive Rower. Stylishly designed and precision built to help you reach peak fitness . . . Variable oar resistance, anatomically designed seat and hydraulic oar brakes. Stores in vertical position ONLY **£129.95** (plus £5 carriage).

J REBOUNDER. The rage that is sweeping America! With the "Rebounder" you can jog, sprint or bounce your way to fitness with a complete course of planned exercises—all in the comfort of your own home. You can even use it watching television! ONLY ———— **£49.95** (plus £5 carriage).

All items available at any of our branches or Mail Order.

physical at Sportsmans

Home Exerciser

A growing number of people take to some sporting activity each year to keep themselves fit. The page opposite shows part of an advertisement for sports equipment.

A1 How much would you have to pay for
    a) an Executive Rower?
    b) a Home Cycle Exerciser?
    c) a Home Rower?
    d) an Executive-Ergonometer Cycle?
  2 'Plus £5 carriage' means add £5 to the cost of the equipment to pay the cost of packing and posting/you get a carriage with the equipment if you pay £5. Which?

Look at A Home Cycle Exerciser
a) The Home Cycle Exerciser comes complete with a speedometer. What else does it have?
b) Why do you think the Home Cycle Exerciser has an alarm?

Look at B Home Rower
  4 Is the Home Rower strongly built or not do you think? Why?
  5 'Variable resistance' means can be made easier or harder to row/can be easily sold. Which?

Look at C Executive Rower
  6 Copy the writing below, changing the underlined words for words from the box which have a similar meaning:
Stylishly designed and precision built to help you reach peak fitness.

well made, maximum, attractive

Look at E Executive-Ergometer Cycle
  7 Copy and complete using *one* of the words in brackets:
a) The cycle was built with the help of medical experts from (Sweden/USA/Finland).
b) A rev counter shows the number of times the _____ has turned. (handles/wheel/saddle).

Look at G Chromium Plated Dumbells
  8 What do dumbells improve?
  9 What do you receive free if you buy four pairs of dumbells?
10 Give the cost (without carriage) of
    a) a 4 kgs pair of dumbells
    b) a 10 kgs pair
    c) a 1 kg pair
11 Give the *total* cost (price + carr.) of
    a) a 9 kgs pair of dumbells
    b) a 3 kgs pair
    c) a 2 kgs pair
    d) a 6 kgs pair
    e) a 8 kgs pair

Look at J Rebounder
12 Name a country where the Rebounder is used.
13 The Rebounder can be used for jogging. Name two other activities it can be used for.
14 How much would you have to pay for a Rebounder (cost and carriage)?
15 All the equipment shown can be bought at Sportsmans stores in Glasgow and Edinburgh. Write the address of the Edinburgh store.

B1 Write a paragraph saying why you think exercise is good for you/not good for you.

Telephone shelf

This shelf clips on to two screw heads projecting from the wall, and is easily removed when decorating. its overall size is 60 cm long × 17 cm high × 31 cm wide. Hang it so the shelf top is 1.05 m above floor level; this is a good height for most people.

Complex shaping and jointing is eliminated by making use of pre-cut mouldings and simple butt-joints.

CONSTRUCTION

Cut shelf (1) and check for square. Cut 45° bevel on one end of side fillets (2) and glue and pin them to underside of shelf, flush with front and sides and projecting at back. Glue front fillet (3) to shelf, flush with front edge.

Glue scotia moulding (4) to projecting ends of side fillets and back edge of shelf.

Cut back panel (5) and check for square. Cut 45° bevel on one end of side fillets (6). Glue and pin them to back panel, flush with top edge and projecting at bottom. Glue and pin top fillet (7) to back panel, flush with top edge.

Glue projecting ends of side fillets and edge of back panel to scotia moulding.

Cut end pieces (8) from one 19 cm × 30

cm from one panel (fig. 2). Glue and pin them in position, flush with edges all round.

Glue quadrant mouldings (9) together in pairs. Glue resulting half-round mouldings to front and top edges of shelf.

Fit keyhole plates to back edges of blocks (10), 1 cm from top, after cutting slots behind keyholes to take screw heads. Glue and screw blocks to back, 6 cm from ends.

Fill and sand all edges and joints, and finish with gloss paint.

Hang shelf on round-headed screws.

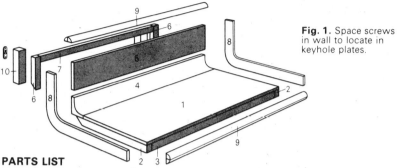

Fig. 1. Space screws in wall to locate in keyhole plates.

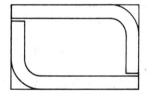

Fig. 2. Cutting end pieces from one panel.

PARTS LIST

No.	Name	Quantity	Long	Wide	Thick	Material
1	Shelf	1	58	23	1	plywood
2	Side fillets	2	25	2	2	softwood
3	Front fillet	1	54	2	2	softwood
4	Scotia moulding	1	58	4	4	ramin
5	Back panel	1	58	8	1	plywood
6	Side fillets	2	10.5	2	2	softwood
7	Top fillet	1	54	2	2	softwood
8	End pieces	2	29	15	1	plywood
9	Quadrant mouldings	4	60	1.5	1.5	ramin
10	Back blocks	2	11	3	3	softwood

HARDWARE: two keyhole plates

Note: dimensions are finished sizes in centimetres, when ordering timber, allow extra for waste.

This lightweight telephone shelf leaves the floor clear and is easily detached.

Designer: David J. Day

Do it Yourself

Some people enjoy making things. To others it's just a chore. The page opposite is from a well-known Do-it-Yourself book which deals with things to make and how to make them.

Look at the first paragraph

1 Give the measurements of the telephone shelf.
2 How high should the shelf top be above floor-level.
3 Why has the shelf-height given opposite been used?

Look at 'Construction'

4 a) What is the first thing you check when you have cut the shelf out?
   b) A bevel is a slope on a piece of wood etc. It is measured in degree (°). How many degrees is the bevel on one end of the side fillets?
5 How are the side fillets fixed on to the shelf?
6 'Flush' means sticking out/level with. Which?
7 a) What is the next thing to be glued to the shelf after the side fillets?
   b) What should the scotia moulding be glued to?
8 What do you glue and pin to the back panel? (Name all parts.)
9 What do you cut the end pieces from?
10 Do you glue quadrant mouldings together in twos, threes or fours?
11 a) Where do you fit keyhole plates?
    b) Why do you cut slots behind keyholes?
12 How far from the ends do you glue and screw blocks?
13 What sort of paint is used to finish the telephone shelf?
14 What should the shelf be hung on?

Look at 'Parts List' and the drawing

15 Copy the drawing if you wish.
16 What are the following parts made of?
   a) the shelf
   b) side fillets
17 What are the numbers of the following parts?
   a) scotia moulding
   b) top fillet
18 How long are the following parts?
   a) part no 2
   b) part no 5
19 How wide are the following parts?
   a) the shelf
   b) the quadrant mouldings

B1 Below are ten points. Five are *for* do-it-yourself, and five against. Write down the five which are for it.

When you Do-it-Yourself you know its been done well.

Do-it-Yourself is cheaper than buying.

I'd rather Do-it-Somebody-else.

Doing it yourself is too much like hard work.

Do-it-Yourself is a useful hobby, and teaches you some skills.

Things look better when they're bought.

Sometimes you can't buy exactly what you want.

You get a good feeling knowing you've made something yourself.

Do-it-Yourself takes too long.

Do-it-Yourself is more expensive than buying once you've paid for your tools.

London's River

Tower of London

Construction of the White Tower commenced in 1078 during the reign of William the Conqueror. Her Majesty's Palace and Fortress of the Tower of London has been added to by succeeding monarchs. In addition to its use as a Royal residence and fortress, the Tower has also been a prison, a place of execution, an armoury, the Royal treasure house, a mint, an observatory, and a zoo.

The Tower covers an area of approximately 18 acres, houses the Crown Jewels and a magnificent collection of armour. Adjacent is Tower Bridge constructed in 1894 and measuring 800 ft. between the two towers. The bridge, the last downstream bridge across the Thames, can be raised and lowered for ships to pass. On the southbank, opposite the Tower of London is HMS Belfast.

Greenwich

The Cutty Sark is a famous clipper, built for the Far East tea trade. There is a museum on board and you can explore the hold and the crew quarters.

Moored nearby is Gypsy Moth IV, the yacht used by Sir Francis Chichester to sail around the World, single handed in 1968.

The Old Royal Observatory at the top of the hill was designed by Sir Christopher Wren. The Meridian 0° line is marked on the side of the building and along the causeway. Here you can stand with one foot in each of the East and West Hemispheres.

The National Maritime Museum which houses relics of English naval history, is situated in the Queen's House and in a range of adjoining buildings.

Construction commenced in 1617 for Anne of Denmark, Consort of King James I — hence the name Queen's House.

The Painted Hall, forming part of the noble group of buildings housing the Royal Naval College, is well worth a visit.

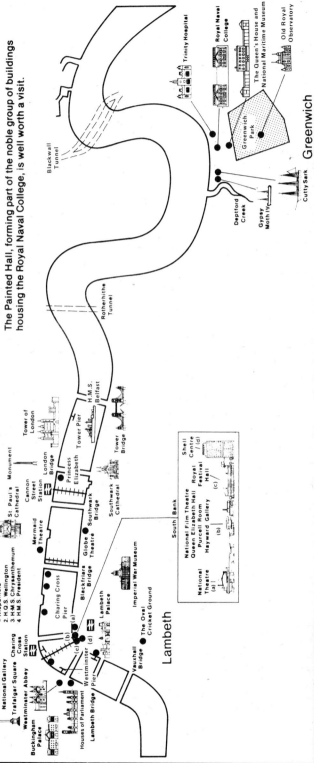

A Trip down the River

Every day boats sail up and down the River Thames in London carrying tourists eager to see the sights. The map opposite shows some of the places of interest which can be found on the banks of the River Thames, and some of the buildings which can be viewed without leaving the boat.

A1 a) How many tunnels can you count under the river?
b) How many railway bridges can you count? (They look like this: ┤┤┤┤┤)
c) How many road bridges can you count?

2 If you look carefully at the map, you will be able to see the names of the road bridges printed by the bridges themselves. Write down all the names you can find.

3 Many famous boats are anchored in the Thames. Some are named, and some are numbered on the map.
a) Copy and complete these named boats:
Princ__ __ __ Eliz__ __ __ __ __
HMS B__ __fa__ __
b) Copy and complete these numbered boats: (look at the key to the left of St. Paul's Cathedral)
No 1 His__ __ __iola
No 2 HQS We__ __ing__ __n
No 3 HMS C__ __ __ __santhem__ __
No 4 HMS Pres__ __ __ __ __

4 Draw this compass:

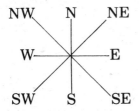

5 Look in the NW (north-west) part of the map.
a) Name the Queen's palace.
b) Name the place where Parliament meets.
c) Name the square which can be found in front of the National Gallery.
d) Name the British Rail station a little to the east (E) of Westminster Abbey.
e) Name the tower a little to the north (N) of Trafalgar Square.

6 Look at the SW (south-west) part of the map;
a) What is the name of the cricket ground?
b) What is the museum called?
c) What is the name of the palace?
d) Name the four buildings which are on the south bank of the River Thames near to Waterloo Bridge—(a) (b) (c) and (d) in the little frame.

7 Look at the north (N) side of the map:
a) Near to which theatre is St. Paul's Cathedral?
b) Name the railway station between Southwark Bridge and London Bridge.
c) Name the famous tower to the east of the Monument.
d) Why is Tower Bridge unusual?

8 Look at the south-east (SE) part of the map:
a) Write the names of the two boats which are anchored near Deptford Creek.
b) What is the name of the hospital and the college close by it?
c) What sort of museum is near the Queen's House?
d) What is the full name of the Observatory in Greenwich Park?

POOLE'S CAVERN is open to the public from Easter until late Autumn. It is usually closed on Wednesdays, except in July and August.

It is a natural cave in which the thief and robber Poole is supposed to have lived around 1440.

Inside is the source of the River Wye.

After some careful digging, bones of animals and men have been discovered in the cave. Iron Age pottery, knives and weapons have also been found and from the Roman Period, more pottery, coins and brooches made of bronze. All the items are on display in the Interpretation Centre at Poole's Cavern.

Today the cave is the home of cave shrimps which have turned white and lost their sight.

Stalactites are cones hanging from the roof of the cave and made by the dripping water as it leaves tiny deposits of lime. When the drip splashes on to the floor another cone is built on the ground. This is called a stalagmite and after many hundreds of years, the two cones may join together to make a pillar.

The first visitors carried candles or wooden torches to light their way and in 1859 —— seventeen gas lamps were fitted. These lasted until 1976 when electricity and the flood lamps were added.

Nobody has ever caught one of the cave's bats, so the species has not yet been identified. They are able to fly in the darkness because they have their own kind of 'radar' system.

The path to the Temple goes up through the woods behind Poole's Cavern.

GRIN LOW is the hill above the cave. The tower on top is SOLOMON's TEMPLE and was built in 1896 by Solomon Mycock to give work to some of Buxton's unemployed. From the top it is possible to see Kinder Scout, Mam Tor and Axe Edge.

A party of soldiers used the top of AXE EDGE to signal to their friends on Lincoln Cathedral and on the top of Snowdon when they were making the early ordnance survey maps. Modern map makers use TRIG POINTS and there is one on the highest point of Axe Edge.

Today, LIMESTONE from Derbyshire is used in more than twenty industries. It was first quarried for use by builders and farmers. Buxton's Roman Bath was made with lime cement and to make fertilizers limestone was burnt in a kiln. The old GRIN QUARRY behind Poole's Cavern has been landscaped and now forms part of the Buxton Country Park.

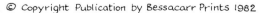

Telephone Doncaster 0302 - 536426

Look at Buxton

Buxton is a well-known holiday town on the edge of the Peak District in Derbyshire. The page opposite is from a booklet which describes the place itself, and some of the interesting things which can be seen round about.

Poole's Cavern

A1 A cavern is a large cave/a rock. Which?

2 Is Poole's cavern open in December?

3 Is the Cavern open on Wednesdays in May?

4 Has the cavern been made by men, or is it a natural cave?

5 Who was Poole? When did he live?

6 Which river starts in the cavern (has its source there)?

7 List the things that have been discovered in the cave.

8 Where are the items which have been found in the cave shown (displayed)?

9 Name *two* animals found in Poole's Cavern.

10 What is made on the roof of the cave by dripping water leaving behind traces of lime?

11 What is made on the cave-floor in the same way?

12 How is a cave pillar made?

13 Copy the drawing of stalactites and stalagmites.

14 If you had entered the cave 100 years ago, how would you have found your way around?

15 How was the cave-lighting changed in 1976?

Grin Low

16 What is 'Grin Low'?

17 Copy the drawing of Solomon's Temple and write 'Solomon's Temple, 1896' under it.

18 Who built the tower? Why did he build it?

19 Can you see Axe Edge from the top of 'Solomon's Temple'?

20 To which two places did soldiers on Axe Edge signal when they were making maps, many years ago?

21 'Trig points' are now used by map-makers. Find the trig-point drawing opposite and copy it.

Limestone

22 In how many industries is limestone used?

23 Who were the first people to dig it out (quarry it)?

24 How were fertilizers made?

25 Landscaped means made an area into a pleasant place once more/escaped from somewhere. Which?

26 What has been landscaped? What is it now part of?

B1 The Peak District is an area of land covering many miles where people can walk, climb, visit caves or just enjoy a picnic in pleasant surroundings. Write a paragraph saying what you would like to do if you spent a day in an area like the Peak District.

Rome and Sorrento

TOUR 108
14 DAYS FROM £200

SORRENTO

Beautiful Sorrento perched above the picturesque harbour is an ideal resort for all ages, with its colourful squares, orange and lemon groves, warm sunny climate and gay romantic evenings. It is ideally situated for excursions to Capri, Naples, Pompeii or spectacular Mount Vesuvius. Your courier will be happy to make suitable arrangements for you.

1st Day — Saturday *North-West — Felixstowe.* We depart from any one of the joining points listed on page two, and travel to Cranage Coach Station. Here we join our tour coach and travel across country to Felixstowe, where we board the night ferry to Zeebrugge. Halts will be made en route for lunch and dinner.

2nd Day — Sunday *Zeebrugge — Reims — Besançon.* We leave the port this morning and motor by way of Bruges to Meenen. Entering France, we proceed through the 1914-18 battlefields at St. Quentin and Reims. Our route then lies through the Upper Vosges across the Langres Plateau to Besançon for dinner and the night.

3rd Day — Monday *Besançon — Stresa.* Today we travel into Switzerland. Passing Lausanne and Montreux we travel along the Rhône Valley, flanked by majestic Swiss mountains, over the Simplon Pass and into Italy. After brief frontier formalities we continue to Lake Maggiore, jewel of the Italian Lakes and our overnight hotel in Stresa.

4th Day — Tuesday *Stresa — Florence.* We leave Stresa and join the Autostrada del Sol to Florence, the great Etruscan city which is a veritable treasure house.

5th Day — Wednesday *Florence — Sorrento.* Our journey continues this morning by Autostrada towards Rome, and on to Sorrento for a stay of three nights at the Hotel St. Lucia.

6th and 7th Days — Thursday/Friday Free in Sorrento. Lunches are not included to allow greater freedom of movement.

8th Day — Saturday *Sorrento — Rome.* Today, we journey towards the Eternal City passing Pompeii and the spectacular Mount Vesuvius en route. We arrive in Rome for a stay of two nights at the Hotel Marco Polo.

Sorrento

9th Day — Sunday At leisure in Rome. Allowing us freedom to visit the many famous places of interest — the Colosseum, Trevi Fountain, St. Peter's and the Vatican, the Forum and the Victor Emmanuel Memorial — by optional excursion.

10th Day — Monday *Rome — Milan.* Retracing our outward route we motor today to Italy's greatest industrial city and home of the world-renowned La Scala Opera House

11th Day — Tuesday *Milan — Pontarlier.* This morning we leave Milan for the Italian Lakes. We re-enter Switzerland over the Simplon Pass to Lake Geneva, Montreux and into France for dinner and the night in Pontarlier.

12th Day — Wednesday *Pontarlier — Paris.* We leave Pontarlier for Dijon and express route to the most romantic city in France. The city for the young at heart. This evening you will thrill to see this sparkling city, so gaily illuminated, and perhaps visit one of the many night clubs.

13th Day — Thursday *Paris — Le Havre.* We depart from this great city this afternoon and join the autoroute to Le Havre, where we halt for dinner before the night crossing to Southampton.

14th Day — Friday *Southampton — Home.* Leaving Southampton we make our way home by the most direct route, stopping en route for breakfast and lunch. On arrival at Cranage we are met by feeder coaches, and returned to our original joining point.

All joining points are listed on page two of the brochure. Detailed itineraries will be provided three weeks prior to departure along with your travel documents.

Inclusive of travel, accommodation, breakfast and dinner on all days. Lunch is not provided on any day.

Please Note: *Tour cost does not include cost of Pullman seats, couchettes or berths on the ferry. These can be booked by your agent at an additional charge.*

Outward sailing: dep, 23.00, arr. 07.00.
Return sailing: dep. 23.00, arr. 07.00.
(Townsend/Thoresen Ferries).

Departing Saturdays	
May 1, September 25, October 2	£200
May 8, September 18	£203
May 15, 22, September 11	£205
May 29, June 5	£208
August 21, 28, September 4	£210
June 12, 19, 26, July 3, 10, August 7, 14	£212
July 17, 24, 31	£215
Single room supplement	£25

Holidays Abroad

Since the 1960s more and more people have been spending some of their free time abroad on holiday. This is because travel and hotel costs have gone down, and because families now bring in more money than they used to. The page opposite is from a holiday booklet advertising coach tours abroad.

A1 Copy and match the words on the left with the meanings on the right:

Picturesque means — areas where orange and lemon trees are found.

Orange and lemon groves are — someone who looks after holidaymakers.

Ideally situated for excursions means — pretty or pleasant to look at.

A courier is — well placed for trips out.

2 Look at the days given on the sheet opposite. How many days does the holiday last for?

3 On which day of the week does
a) the holiday begin?
b) the coach *reach* Florence?
c) the coach *arrive* in Rome?
d) the coach *reach* Paris?
e) the holiday finish

4 Which town or city does the coach *leave* on the
a) 4th day?   b) 11th day?
c) 12th day? d) 13th day?

5 a) Which days of the week are 'free' in Sorrento?
b) Which day of the week is 'free' (at leisure) in Rome?

6 On which day of the week could you see:
a) The Rhône Valley?
b) Mount Vesuvius?
c) The Trevi Fountain?
d) La Scala Opera House?

7 a) Where would you have dinner on the 2nd day?
b) What is the name of the pass you would go over on the 3rd day?
c) What is the name of the lake you would see on the 3rd day?
d) Which hotel would you begin your stay at on the 5th day?
e) Which Roman city would you pass on your 8th day?
f) Where do you cross to on the 13th day?

8 Look at the box in the bottom right-hand corner of the page opposite.
a) What is the cost of the holiday if you want to travel on May 15th?
b) What is the cost if you wish to travel on August 21st?

B1 Below are six points for and against going abroad by coach. Write down the three points which are *against* such a holiday.

Travelling by coach is fine — the driver does all the work.

Travelling by coach makes you feel sick.

Modern coaches are fast and comfortable.

I like to plan my own holiday — not let someone else plan it for me.

On coach holidays you can make friends and meet people.

I'd rather just fly somewhere and then stay put.

6-8 BERTH TILLER-STEERED NARROWBOAT

Diagram showing open stern deck

Length 15.5 m; Beam 2 m; Headroom 1.9 m.
Two boats, both with open stern deck, built 1980.
Three cabins with shower, two flushing W.C.'s and two handbasins. The first and second cabins are separated by a W.C. and shower and the second and third by a W.C. and the galley.

The forward cabin can accommodate 2 persons in a double berth or up to 4 persons in single berths.

The middle cabin provides a large seating area and a folding table is supplied for dining. It can accommodate 2 persons in a double berth or two-tier bunks. There is access to the outside through side doors.

The after cabin has a raised dinette that easily converts to a double berth.

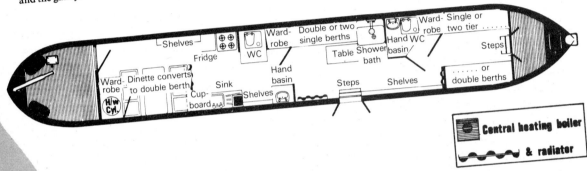

INVENTORY

GALLEY EQUIPMENT

1 Frying Pan
3 Saucepans
1 Casserole
1 Kettle
1 Tea Pot
1 Milk Jug
1 Measuring Jug
1 Sugar Bowl
1 Butter Dish
1 Bread Bin
1 Bread Board
1 Bread Knife
2 Kitchen Knives
1 Chopping Board
1 Cruet Set
1 Ladle
1 Serving Spoon
1 Fish Slice
1 Masher
1 Wooden Spoon
1 Potato Peeler
1 Cheese Grater
1 Rolling Pin
1 Mixing Bowl
1 Pie Dish
1 Baking Tin
1 Roasting Tin
1 Colander
1 Tin Opener
1 Bottle Opener
1 Cork Screw
1 Ashtray
1 Draining Rack
1 Washing-up Bowl

CLEANING EQUIPMENT

1 Broom
1 Mop
1 Scrubbing Brush
1 Lavatory Brush
1 Dustpan and Brush
1 Bucket
1 Floor Cloth
1 Dish Cloth
2 Tea Towels

CROCKERY AND CUTLERY

Dinner Plates
Tea Plates
Bowls
Cups and Saucers
Mugs
Glasses
Wine Glasses
Egg Cups
Knives
Forks
Spoons
Tea Spoons

(Above items in quantities of 6, 8, 10 and 14 according to boat size)

BEDDING

3 Blankets per Berth
1 Pillow and Case per Berth

NAVIGATION EQUIPMENT

1 Boarding Plank
2 Mooring Ropes
2 Mooring Spikes
1 Heavy Hammer
3 Windlasses (for locks)
1 Boathook
1 Long Pole
1 Hose and Reel
1 Large Magnet
1 Stanley Knife
1 Radiator Key
Set of Waterproofs
Keys and Padlock
Instruction Manual
1 Deck Scrubber

Holidays Afloat

Canals in Britain were first made to carry goods from one town to another. Now, however, they are mainly used for leisure. The clip opposite is from a booklet advertising boating holidays. The boats used are narrowboats — the same sort of vessel that carried goods a hundred years ago.

A1 Draw the diagram of the narrowboat.

Look at the information given in the top left-hand corner of the page

2 Below are a number of sentences about the narrowboat. Some are true and some are false. Copy the sentences which are true.

    The boat was built in 1982.
    Three cabins have a shower.
    There are three handbasins.
    The forward cabin will accommodate 10 people.
    There is a folding table for dining.
    There is no after cabin.

3 Copy and match the words on the left with the meanings on the right.

H/W Cyl   is a toilet.
WC   is a sleeping place on a ship or boat.
A berth   is a hot-water cylinder.

Look at 'Inventory'

4 Copy the list of items below and tick (✓) the ones you would find in the galley (Galley Equipment).
1 bread knife, 1 lavatory brush, dinner plates, 1 ladle, 1 cheese grater, 1 pillow, 1 washing-up bowl, 2 tea towels, 1 serving spoon, bowls, forks, 1 heavy hammer, keys and padlock, 1 deck scrubber, 1 milk jug

5 Copy the items below and tick the ones you can find under 'Cleaning Equipment'.
1 masher, mugs, 1 boarding plank, 1 bucket, 2 tea towels, 1 map, 1 sugar bowl, 1 frying pan, 1 long pole, 1 radiator key, 1 Stanley knife, 1 dish cloth

6 Make two lists. Head one 'Crockery and Cutlery'. Head the other 'Navigation Equipment'. Put the words below under the correct heading: teaspoons, 1 hose and reel, 2 mooring spikes, egg cups, 3 windlasses, 1 large magnet, tea plates, glasses, wine glasses, 1 boathook, set of waterproofs, spoons

B1 Write a paragraph saying why you would like/would not like to spend a holiday on a canal narrowboat.

Miniature Golf

HIGH PEAK
DEPARTMENT OF TOURISM AND LEISURE
MINIATURE GOLF SCORE CARD

Hole No.	Score	Hole No.	Score
1	2	Total*	21
2	3	10	3
3	4	11	3
4	4	12	1
5	1	13	3
6	1	14	1
7	2	15	4
8	2	16	4
9	2	17	1
Total*	21	18	3
		TOTAL SCORE	44

RULES OF PLAY

1. The ball to be holed in the fewest possible strokes. Each stroke counts as a point. The lowest scorer is the winner.
2. Should the ball not be holed on the first stroke, succeeding strokes to be taken from where the ball stops.
3. Should the ball be unplayable, being too near the edge or right in front of an obstacle, it may be moved up to 8 inches towards the centre.
4. Should the ball jump the rink:
   a) before an obstacle, then the ball is to be played anew from the tee.
   b) behind an obstacle, then the ball is to be played from the point it left the course.
5. Should the ball run back behind the tee point, then it is to be played from the tee.
6. Should the player fail to hole out in 7 strokes his score-card is to be marked 8 for this hole. The game then continues from the next tee.
7. Each hole is to be played in succession as numbered.

NOTES: The rink itself is not to be trodden or walked upon. The golf clubs are only for the personal use of the players engaged, and on leaving the course the player is to return the clubs and balls to the attendant. Damage and loss to be made good by the player responsible.

Miniature Golf Score Card

A1 a) How many holes were taken with a score of 1?
b) How many holes were taken with a score of 2?
c) How many with a score of 3?
d) How many with a score of 4?
e) What was the total score?

Rules of Play

2 **Rule 1** — Who is the winner of the game — the highest or the lowest scorer?

3 **Rule 2** — Where are the other strokes to be taken from if the ball is not holed in the first stroke?

4 **Rule 3** — If a ball is unplayable, how far from an obstacle may it be moved?

5 **Rule 4** — Where is a ball to be played from if it goes out of the ground (jumped the rink) *behind* an obstacle?

6 **Rule 5** — Where is a ball which has run back behind the tee point to be played from?

7 **Rule 6** — What score is written on the card of a player who fails to hole out in 7 strokes?

8 **Rule 7** — Can you play the holes in any order, or must they be played as numbered?